Moosings
of a Cow

21 Life Lessons from the Barnyard

DARREN J. SQUIRE

Trilogy Christian Publishers
A Wholly Owned Subsidary of Trinity Broadcasting Network
2442 Michelle Drive
Tustin, CA 92780

For information, address Trilogy Christian Publishing
Rights Department, 2442 Michelle Drive, Tustin, Ca 92780.
Trilogy Christian Publishing/ TBN and colophon are trademarks of Trinity Broadcasting Network.

For information about special discounts for bulk purchases, please contact Trilogy Christian Publishing.

Manufactured in the United States of America

10 9 8 7 6 5 4 3 2 1

Library of Congress Cataloging-in-Publication Data is available.

ISBN 979-8-88738-137-4 (Print Book)
ISBN 979-8-88738-138-1 (ebook)

Dedication

To my father, Major James M. Squire:

I could not ask for a better dad. You have always been there for us. You are man of great integrity, strength, and honor. You emulated our Father in Heaven and gave me the two greatest blessings of my life: to know the Lord Jesus and to have the most wonderful family here on Earth. From you, I learned my honor and integrity. You were a hero in the time that you served our great nation, but you were also a hero to our family and to me. I love you.

To my mother, Kathleen B. Squire:

Mom, you have always been there for me. I could not ask for a better mother. From my first memories, you taught me about the Lord, and gave me my greatest blessing. You have always served our Lord with love and graciousness. You are brilliant, yet humble. From you, I learned my creativity and humor, my faith and my love. You are the best mom that any child could have. You set my feet upon this path, teaching me about Lord, how to honor and love Him with all that He made us to be, and how to love others even as He loves us. I thank you and honor you. I love you.

To my brother, Pastor Jeff Squire:

A man could not have a better brother. We have had the most awesome parents. I believe that our lives have turned out in a manner worthy of their sacrifice and love. I know that yours has. You have always been there for me. I remember everything from the beginning when you were first born. And we have shared many wonderful adventures. You are the most loyal, loving, skilled, and honorable man that I know. You have become the best pastor, serving our Father in Heaven perfectly according to His perfect will. I have personally witnessed you to be the best husband, pastor, friend, and soon-to-be father. I so greatly admire you and call myself blessed that I have you as my brother, not just by blood, but mainly in faith together in the Lord Jesus. I love you.

Acknowledgments

I wish to acknowledge my father, James M. Squire, as the inspiration for my book. In 2012, we nearly lost him because of a heart condition. He had an emergency aortic valve replacement, which was replaced by a cow valve. We were told that it was a miracle that he was even around for the heart surgery to take place. From a place of stress, we sort of teased you about the cow valve in order to alleviate the stress. My mom was the first, but I quickly picked up on it. For ten years, you have endured my teasing and cow jokes, with everyone else piling on, and you have done so with great magnanimity, even adding to it yourself. You are such a great dad! So then I thought, why not be more serious with this. And so we are here. This is the personal fulfilment of Genesis 50:20, "But as for you, ye thought evil against me; but God meant it unto good, to bring to pass, as it is this day, to save much people alive," and also Romans 8:28, "And we know that all things work together for good to them that love God, to them who are the called according to *his* purpose." You are here with us today dad. I hope to honor you.

1. Be the bull, not a bully.

The bull protects the herd. The bully harasses them.
The bull charges the way forward. The bully slows the herd down.
Being the bull means that you are strong. Being the bully means you are weak.

2. The grass isn't always greener on the other side of the fence.

The grass over there looks so fresh, yours looks stale.
The grass over there looks so bucolic, yours seems so urban.
The grass over there looks so green, yours seems artificial.
Is that grass over there really exceptional, or are you just
    bored with yours?
Be thankful for each blade that you can enjoy. That grass over
    there may not be what you think.

6

3. Run with the bulls, not from them.

The bull seems intimidating.
The bull seems unapproachable.
The bull may be one of a kind in the herd, but don't run
    away from him.
Learn from him.
Emulate him.
Run with him.

4. Reach for the stars. You may just jump over the moon.

Each night, every cow sees the moon and dreams.
But as the sun rises, the dream fades into the barnyard routine.
Don't be just another heifer that just dreams for the moon.
Be the bold bovine that the reaches for the stars!
You may just then jump over the moon!

5. You can hit the broad side of a barn.

Most other cows may just be happy being milked.
Most other cows may just be happy chewing the cud all the time.
Most other cows may just be happy mooing all day.
But don't be just like most other cows who never take a shot.
They say you can't hit it, but you can hit the broad side of that barn.

6. Be careful of chasing the flashy red cape. There can be danger behind it.

Sometimes things just catch your attention.
That flashy red cape seems so unusual.
That flashy red cape seems so captivating.
You are just drawn to it.
But beware, what's behind it may stick it to you.

7. Don't leave the runt out of the herd.

Each member of the herd has dreams.
Each member of the herd has fears.
But each member of the herd has different abilities.
Abilities to achieve the dreams and conquer the fears.
Be kind the runt, because he is part of the herd, and not every
     cow is kind to him.

8. Sometimes you need a thick hide.

Not all animals in the barnyard are kind.
The chickens may nitpick at you.
The horses ignore you,
And the pigs may throw mudballs at you.
You may need to toughen your hide.

9. Don't let the herd follow the turkey.

A turkey doesn't belong in the field.
A few cows follow to see what's up.
Then, others follow because it's the thing to do.
Soon the whole herd is following the turkey.
Are you a follower or a leader?
Maybe you too will just follow the turkey.

20

10. Be careful of your rump or it could get roasted.

The pasture may be safe.
The pasture may be peaceful.
But it's still good to watch your back.
Otherwise, your rump may get roasted.

11. Hang around the pigs, and you may get muddy.

The pigs don't live in the pasture, but the mudhole.
They may seem fun,
But they don't mind being muddy.
Hang around them, and you'll get muddy too.

12. Take time to chew the cud.

Sometimes you don't always have to be charging ahead.
Sometimes you should just rest in the field.
Sometimes just relax, think and chew the cud.

13. Don't cry over spilled milk.

Life in the barn isn't always bucolic.
You may be doing your best,
But sometimes the milk still gets spilled.
You shouldn't cry over it.
Accept it and enjoy the peaceful pasture.

14. Don't tailgate. You'll start a stampede.

Being part of the herd doesn't mean tailgating.
Each cow may have four stomachs, but also has a brain.
Don't blindly follow the next cow too closely,
Or you may crash into him and start a stampede.

15. Being a heifer sometimes means tap dancing.

Sometimes a situation requires finesse.
A cow must be delicate.
A little shuffle here of the hooves.
A small side step there.
You can naturally tap dance around any problem.

16. Don't toot your own horn.

No one likes a snob.
You may be one fantastic bovine.
But let others see it.
You don't have to rub their noses in it.
You shouldn't toot your own horn.

17. Beware of tall tales.

Every cow has a story to tell.
Some tails may be longer than others though.
Be wise in what you and who you believe.
Be truthful in what you tell.
No BS. Be authentic.

18. Sometimes you must take the bull by the horns.

The herd will generally follow the bull.
But sometimes he will lead the herd the wrong way.
The bull doesn't really like to be told where to go.
If he leads the wrong way, you must sometimes take him by
      the horns, and steer him the right way.

38

19. It's good to be a cash cow.

It is good to be productive.
Each of us has unique talents and gifts.
Develop your talents.
Be open to opportunity,
And become your own cash cow.

20. Try not to be a bull in a China shop.

While it may be good to be charging at times,
Other situations require finesse.
Know your limitations, your strengths and weaknesses.
If you are not, you may not be matched with your place.
You could cause a lot of damage.

42

21. Wait until the cows come home.

Life doesn't move to our own schedule.
We like to charge ahead and get things done.
We want immediate results.
We don't like to wait for others,
But patience is a forgotten virtue.
Learn to wait peacefully until the cows come home.

About the Author

Author Darren J. Squire believes in achieving the utmost potential in this life that the Lord has given us. He is physicist, business owner, world-traveler, and now writer. Having two masters' degrees and working across multiple disciplines, he actively lives out the motto that you must cross-pollinate to innovate. His mission is to seek out as many accounts of human experience so that he may better understand the world around us all, in order to be appreciative of the manifold blessing that have been bestowed upon us all and to be an effective force for good in as many lives as possible, according to the will of the Lord. He sees in as part of discovery of the world around us all, because only once understanding is achieved, more effective action may be taken.

Currently, he studies the Russian language in order to better reach out to that part of the world. Having been to Ukraine 4 times, he has a heart for the people there, particularly in this great hour of need. Knowing that Ukraine has been the traditional breadbasket for Europe and the Soviet Union, he believes that it can become a spiritual breadbasket for the world promoting the gospel of Jesus Christ.

In his leisure time he enjoys traveling, bowling, golf, and generally having a new adventure. He is currently training to eventually climb Mt. Kilimanjaro, but first all the peaks in California. But most importantly, is being with family. He greatly values his family, including all who are family in the Lord.

Printed in the USA
CPSIA information can be obtained
at www.ICGtesting.com
LVHW070906050823
754424LV00033B/137

9 798887 381374